Persistent
P O E M S

A compilation of
prophetic poems to awaken
a deceived generation.

Coleen,

　　　Jesus Loves you
　　　　　Vicky Ash

V I C K Y   A S H

FIRST EDITION

ISBN (Paperback): 978-1739192112

Persistent Poems - Vicky Ash

For more information, please direct your emails to: info@ibelieveican.co.uk

PUBLISHING

DEDICATION

I dedicate Persistent Poems
to Jesus Christ who died for me
and my friends and family
desiring others to be *free*.

CONTENTS

THE WORD OF GOD

Alert is the Word laid on my heart.
Sober-minded,
awake from the start.

Deceptive days
in which we live. Knowing Jesus,
the truth He gives.

Ears to hear.
Eyes to see.
This spiritual war.
Bind the enemy.

1 PETER 5:8-9

[8] Be alert and of sober mind.
Your enemy the devil prowls around like a roaring
lion looking for someone to devour.

[9] Resist him, standing firm in the faith, because you
know that the family of believers throughout the world
is undergoing the same kind of sufferings.

LIGHTING UP THE DARKNESS

Don't look at the dark
I hear men say.
How then do we
expose SRA?

So many children,
groomed and hidden.
Voices silenced.
Justice forbidden.

Suffer the little children
to come unto Me.
We will declare,
My Victory.

EPHESIANS 5:11-12

[11] Have nothing to do with the fruitless deeds
of darkness, but rather expose them.

[12] It is shameful even to mention what
the disobedient do in secret.

SUFFER THE LITTLE CHILDREN

Can you hear the children's cries?
Trafficked, abused, I wonder why?

Hollywood or Hollyrude.
Why is TV now so lewd?
Blasphemy accepted,
the norm, to be crude.

Paedophilia rife.
Murders, rape,
addiction to drugs,
to help one escape.

Evil now good and good is evil.
God help us all!
Could it be the devil?

Does that shock you to the core?
Pray for the children whose voices we ignore.

They suffer in silence.
Where can they go?
The authorities, you say.
I don't think so.

Cover-ups seem common,
to protect the elite.
It's time we asked questions
What do you think?

LUKE 18:16

'But Jesus called the children to him and said,
"Let the little children come to me, and do not hinder them,
for the kingdom of God belongs to such as these.

CHILD PROTECTION

Why do we need
to 'protect' our children
from dark forces that
lead them astray?

Have you thought
we have an enemy
seeking to devour
every day?

The battle we fight
is not flesh and blood.
But spiritual forces
in the unseen world.

With Holy Spirit
the veil is lifted.
Faith is our shield
and the Word is our sword.

EPHESIANS 6:10-12

[10] Finally, be strong in the Lord and in his mighty power.

[11] Put on the full armour of God, so that you can take your stand against the devil's schemes.

[12] For our struggle is not against flesh and blood, but against the rulers, against the authorities, against the powers of this dark world and against the spiritual forces of evil in the heavenly realms.

ENOUGH

We are called to raise our children
in this world full of sin.
Not the state with its agenda,
deceiving them to lure them in.

They are gifts to us from heaven,
redeemed by His precious blood.
Surrendering them all to Jesus
for His protection and perfect love.

Speak up. Let your voice be heard.
Protect their innocence and be tough.
This could be the generation
that will definitely say *"enough!"*

PROVERBS 31:8

⁸ Speak up for those who cannot speak for themselves,
for the rights of all who are destitute.

PRAYERS

Never underestimate
The power of prayer.
In Jesus' name,
decree and declare.

The Word of God,
alive and active.
Over every situation,
not being passive.

HEBREWS 4:12

[12] For the word of God is alive and active.
Sharper than any double-edged sword,
it penetrates even to dividing soul and spirit, joints and marrow;
it judges the thoughts and attitudes of the heart.

LAUREN

No longer in torment
or feeling the pain.
You've gone home.
He knows your name.

Alf, Bruno and Iris, your world,
They will hear of you often.
You're never forgotten.

Your Mum, Dad and siblings too,
loved you more
than I think you knew.

Your cousins reflect on the good old days,
when you would dress up
and play your games.

We miss your laugh and gentle soul.
Give Grandma a hug from us all.

JOHN 14:2-3

2 My Father's house has many rooms; if that were not so,
would I have told you that I am going
there to prepare a place for you?

3 And if I go and prepare a place for you, I will come back
and take you to be with me that you also may be where I am.

SHINE A LIGHT

Everything hidden
will be disclosed.
Satan's agenda
is being exposed.

Many survivors
are speaking out.
Faith with action,
standing out.

"Revenge is mine,"
says the Lord.
"Walk in the light
of my Word."

All who doubt
the truth will see.
Jesus reigns
for eternity

JAMES 2:17

[17] In the same way, faith by itself,
if it is not accompanied by action, is dead.

TIME

Time is precious,
spend it wisely.
Seeking truth,
giving God your diary.

ECCLESIASTES 3:1

[1] There is a time for everything, and a season for every activity under the heavens.

TRUTH IN YOUR WORDS

It is not another's
story to tell.
When it's yours,
it is told so well.

Truth doesn't change.
It stands firm.
Throughout all trials
it will be confirmed.

God will vindicate
those who are His.
In His perfect time.
Trust in this.

ISAIAH 54:17

[17] "No weapon forged against you will prevail,
and you will refute every tongue that accuses you.
This is the heritage of the servants of the Lord,
and this is their vindication from me,"
declares the Lord.

JESUS REIGNS

No matter what the future holds,
Jesus reigns, His story is foretold.

Many suffer in His name
He alone bore their pain.

His grace is sufficient in our weakness.
Perfecting holiness, showing meekness.

Forgive them, they know not what they do.
Victory reigns for those who do.

2 CORINTHIANS 12:9

[9] But He said to me, "My grace is sufficient for you, for my power is made perfect in weakness." Therefore I will boast all the more gladly about my weaknesses, so that Christ's power may rest on me.

CLOSER LORD

Closer Lord, closer to Thee.
Only You open blind eyes to see.

Faith comes by hearing the Word.
Revelation for a dying world.

Wide awake Your plan unfolding.
Trusting You and Your glory beholding.

ROMANS 10:17

¹⁷ Consequently, faith comes from hearing the message, and the message is heard through the word about Christ.

FOLLOW GOD'S CALL

Hearing God's voice
or wanting man's choice?
is really the question
to ask in this season.

Surrendering all
to follow His call
we walk through the fire
pulled out of the mire.

As God brings to light
what is done out of sight,
He will ask us to stand
for freedom in our land.

JOHN 10:27-30

²⁷ My sheep listen to my voice;
I know them, and they follow me.

²⁸ I give them eternal life, and they shall never perish; no one
will snatch them out of my hand.

²⁹ My Father, who has given them to me, is greater than all;
no one can snatch them out of my Father's hand.

³⁰ I and the Father are one."

KEEPING FAITH

The fear of the Lord
is the beginning of wisdom.

The mind of Christ,
exposing deception.

Seek His Word.
Bold faith in this season.

PROVERBS 9:10

[10] The fear of the Lord is the beginning of wisdom,
and knowledge of the Holy One is understanding.

VICTORY IS HIS

The battle belongs
to the Lord
at Calvary's cross.
The Spirit, His Sword.

His timing perfect
and promise sealed
as all wickedness
is revealed.

He gives His glory
to no man.
It will be the work
of His Spirit alone.

'Not by might
nor by power,
but by My Spirit,'
in this hour.

The reason.
The Son of God appeared,
to destroy Satan's work
and we all cheered.

ZECHARIAH 4:6

⁶ So He said to me, "This is the word of the Lord to Zerubbabel: 'Not by might nor by power, but by my Spirit,' says the Lord Almighty.

FOCUS UNWAVERING

Keep your eyes on Jesus
no matter where you are.
Life so very precious
we need His daily care.

Don't trust in man's opinion.
Read His daily Word.
The truth is there to guide us
and little faith is stirred.

PROVERBS 4:25-27

[25] Let your eyes look straight ahead;
fix your gaze directly before you.

WALK WITH THE LORD

Divine connections every day.
When you're walking
Jesus' way.

God's handiwork,
His creation.
Prepared in advance
for salvation.

EPHESIANS 2:10

[10] For we are God's handiwork, created in Christ Jesus to do good works, which God prepared in advance for us to do.

WE NEED CHOICE

No freedom without a vaccine?
Is that the price we pay?
The blood of Jesus covers me
each and every day.

My health is under scrutiny.
Clots I've had before.
Fragmin harmed my baby.
I cannot conform.

Other meds are an alternative.
Let us have a choice.
All things are possible
if you use your voice.

EXODUS 12:13

13 The blood will be a sign for you on the houses where you are, and when I see the blood, I will pass over you. No destructive plague will touch you when I strike Egypt.

LEADER IN GOD

A Godly leader
knows The Way
shows The Way
and goes The Way.
There is no other way.

JOHN 14:6

[6] Jesus answered, "I am the way and the truth and the life.
No one comes to the Father except through me."

BE ALERT

When you're awake
you know what's fake.
News to control
and own your soul.

Truth will unfold
as it is told.
Choices to make
for Heaven's sake.

1 PETER 1:13

¹³ Therefore, with minds that are alert and fully sober, set your hope on the grace to be brought to you when Jesus Christ is revealed at His coming.

BASK IN HIS LOVE

Why so downcast
oh, my soul?
Inner wounds not yet
made whole.

Rise up.
Rise up and follow Thee.
Each step of faith
will set me free.

Loving Jesus
as He loves me.
Walking with Him
to eternity.

PSALMS 147:3

³ He heals the broken-hearted and binds up their wounds.

MADE IN GOD'S IMAGE

Made in God's image.
Divine destiny.
Serving each other
in ministry.

Each on a journey
seeking truth.
Encountering Jesus
and bearing fruit.

The life of God
will never die.
Seek His presence.
Rebuke every lie.

GENESIS 1:27

[27] So God created mankind in his own image, in the image of God He created them; male and female He created them.

FILLED WITH THE WORD

Fill my mind
with God's Word.
It heals my heart
and is my sword.

Rightly dividing
soul and spirit.
Led by Him
without limit.

Declaring truth
and rebuking lies.
Landing me safe
on Canaan's side.

1 THESSALONIANS 5:23-24

23 May God himself, the God of peace, sanctify you through and through. May your whole spirit, soul and body be kept blameless at the coming of our Lord Jesus Christ.

[24] The one who calls you is faithful, and He will do it.

DAILY FAITH

Faith is not felt,
it is received.

We turn from sin
that once deceived.

It's not about the time
we pray.

It is the faith
we use each day.

ACTS 26:17C-18

17c I am sending you to them

18 to open their eyes and turn them from darkness to light, and from the power of Satan to God, so that they may receive forgiveness of sins and a place among those who are sanctified by faith in me.'

THE WAY

I *AM* The Way
The Truth and
The Life.
I AM coming back.
I AM alive.

REVELATION 22:20

[20] He who testifies to these things says,
"Yes, I am coming soon."
Amen. Come, Lord Jesus.

RIGHT LANE

REVELATION

Revelation
is what we need.
To discern the times
and sow God's seed.

His people die through
lack of knowledge.
Truth will birth true faith
and courage.

Godly counsel
transforms lives.
And breaks the chains
of deception and lies.

A new life in Christ
is the perfect escape.
From darkness to light
and heaven awaits.

HOSEA 4:6A

[6a] ...my people are destroyed from lack of knowledge.

OUR PRAYERS ARE ANSWERED

Make good use
of every opportunity.
Declare His truth and
ultimate victory.

Preach the cross of Christ
and Him crucified.
There is the power,
there's no need to hide.

Demons flee
at the sound of His name.
The battle is won so
lift up the lame.

Heaven assists us
with our prayers.
They are yes and amen to
all the sayers.

EPHESIANS 5:15-16

[15] Be very careful, then, how you live—
not as unwise but as wise,

[16] making the most of every opportunity,
because the days are evil.

HIS CULTURE

Cancel culture.
Toxic words.
Unfolding plan.
The spirit of the world.

Jesus culture.
Wise words.
His plan.
Redeeming the world.

1 CORINTHIANS 2:12

¹² What we have received is not the spirit of the world, but the Spirit who is from God, so that we may understand what God has freely given us.

GOD'S PEOPLE WILL RISE

Urgent days
need radical ways.
Keep your eyes on Jesus
to see through the haze.

There is no faith
without action.
God's people are called
to rise to the occasion.

Be bold speaking truth,
no compromise.
We are called to expose
all Satan's lies.

Our God reigns
over heaven and earth.
He sent His spirit
to walk in new birth.

1 PETER 1:3-5

3 Praise be to the God and Father of our Lord Jesus Christ!
In his great mercy, he has given us new birth into a living hope
through the resurrection of Jesus Christ from the dead,

4 and into an inheritance that can never perish, spoil or fade.
This inheritance is kept in heaven for you,

5 who through faith are shielded by God's power until the
coming of the salvation that is ready to
be revealed in the last time.

SEEK THE TRUTH

When you've grown up
in deception.
You seek the truth
and its reflection.

By their fruit
you recognise them.
Standing firm
against all temptation.

It is the sovereign
work of Christ.
To redeem a life
that once lived in strife.

Do not refuse
Him who speaks.
Only the Kingdom
you should seek.

HEBREWS 12:25

[25] See to it that you do not refuse him who speaks.
If they did not escape when they refused him
who warned them on earth, how much less will we,
if we turn away from him who warns us from heaven?

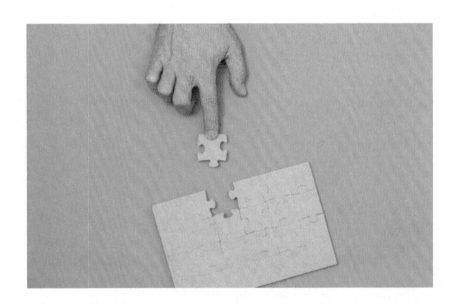

VICKY ASH

I WALK HIS WAY

Everything I am today
Is because God's shown me the way.

Look to Him for all you need.
He will plant in you His seed.

Water it every day,
with His Word and go His way.

You will never thirst again
in a dry and barren land.

JOHN 4:14

¹⁴ But whoever drinks the water I give them will never thirst. Indeed, the water I give them will become in them a spring of water welling up to eternal life."

HE BANISHES TROUBLES

No matter how hard life gets,
God equips all His saints.

If we give our lives to Him,
He will change us from within.

No matter what comes our way,
He will deliver us on that day.

We will have trouble in the world.
That is why God gave His Word.

JOHN 16:33

[33] "I have told you these things, so that in me you may have peace. In this world, you will have trouble. But take heart! I have overcome the world."

EXPOSING EVIL

I've spoken out all my life,
exposing evil that is rife.

Jesus came with a mission;
to destroy the devil and his vision.

It's time to act upon our faith,
not shrink back in distaste.

Apart from Him we can do nothing.
But through Him everything.

His kingdom will never be destroyed.
Arise with faith and be saved.

He alone will draw the remnant,
of His people who are penitent.

HEBREWS 10:36-39

³⁶ You need to persevere so that when you have done the will of God, you will receive what He has promised.

³⁷ For, "In just a little while, He who is coming will come and will not delay."

³⁸ And, "But my righteous one will live by faith. And I take no pleasure in the one who shrinks back."

³⁹ But we do not belong to those who shrink back and are destroyed, but to those who have faith and are saved.

WHAT'S IN YOUR HEART?

Awake or fake?
Time will tell.
God alone
knows man so well.

Hearts of flesh.
Hearts of stone.
Only *He*
transforms each one.

Led by Him,
peace and rest.
Faith over fear
is the test.

EZEKIEL 11:19-20A

¹⁹ I will give them an undivided heart and put a new spirit in them; I will remove from them their heart of stone and give them a heart of flesh.

^{20a} Then they will follow my decrees and be careful to keep my laws.

YOUR VOICE MAKES A DIFFERENCE

Will your voice
make a difference,
in all the controversy
that you witness?

Will you speak
despite persecution,
the Truth of God's Word
to find a solution?

Look beyond
what you can see
and let God show you
what He sees.

To break our hearts
for what breaks His.
This is the only
way to live.

If you want
to change your life.
Repent and believe.
Live for Christ.

ACTS 15:26

²⁶ Men who have risked their lives for the name of our Lord
Jesus Christ.

THE ULTIMATE PRIZE

We all want to be on the winning side
It takes sacrifice keeping your eyes on the prize.

Many are called but few are chosen
Will your life be your daily devotion?

Whoever finds their life will lose it.
and loses their life for His sake will find it.

The only words I long to hear,
"Well done good and faithful servant you are welcome here."

MATTHEW 25:21

²¹ "His master replied, 'Well done, good and faithful servant!
You have been faithful with a few things;
I will put you in charge of many things.
Come and share your master's happiness!'

GOD'S CREATION

Apart from Me
you can do nothing.
Only in Christ
has death lost its sting.

Only when you
cry out to Me,
will I intervene
and set you free.

I alone
satisfy the human heart
which I created
from the start.

JOHN 15:5

[5] "I am the vine; you are the branches. If you remain in me and I in you, you will bear much fruit; apart from me, you can do nothing.

JESUS BY MY SIDE

I know that Jesus, You hold my hand.
All other ground is sinking sand.
My life is hidden now in Christ.
Paid for by Your sacrifice.
Calvary the victory.
The greatest day in history.
Not my will but Yours be done.
Until the time You call me home.

COLOSSIANS 3:1-4

¹ Since, then, you have been raised with Christ, set your hearts on things above, where Christ is, seated at the right hand of God.

² Set your minds on things above, not on earthly things.

³ For you died, and your life is now hidden with Christ in God.

⁴ When Christ, who is your life, appears, then you also will appear with him in glory.

SAVED FROM FEAR

Speaking the truth
to those held dear.
The Word of life
saves men from fear.

Our fight is not against
flesh and blood.
It is a spiritual war
won only in love.

Blind eyes see
and deaf ears hear,
the work of Holy Spirit
when Jesus draws near.

EPHESIANS 4:15

¹⁵ Instead, speaking the truth in love, we will grow to become in every respect the mature body of him who is the head, that is, Christ.

CREATED ANEW

Whenever your story
is all about you.
There's more in your life
for God to do.

He comforts you
to comfort others,
with the same comfort
His spirit offers.

In Christ you are
a new creation.
Redeemed and saved.
No more condemnation.

He restores the years
the locusts have eaten,
and gives to you
the joy of salvation.

Christ in you,
the hope of glory.
Shine for Him,
not your story.

2 CORINTHIANS 1:3-4

³ Praise be to the God and Father of our Lord Jesus Christ, the Father of compassion and the God of all comfort,

⁴ who comforts us in all our troubles, so that we can comfort those in any trouble with the comfort we ourselves receive from God.

SERVING CHRIST ALWAYS

Changed by the power
of God's Word.
As evil increases
do not stay in the world.

Kingdom perspective
in these days.
Serving Christ
in all His ways.

COLOSSIANS 3:23-24

[23] Whatever you do, work at it with all your heart, as working for the Lord, not for human masters,

[24] since you know that you will receive an inheritance from the Lord as a reward. It is the Lord Christ you are serving

BE THE CHANGE

Those in authority,
in the spotlight,
failing children
out of sight.

It's time corruption
is exposed.
To rescue
every one of those.

Love compels
me every day,
to step out in faith
and make a way.

PROVERBS 31:8-9

⁸ Speak up for those who cannot speak for themselves,
for the rights of all who are destitute.

⁹ Speak up and judge fairly;
defend the rights of the poor and needy.

WALK WITH HIM

Profoundly changed,
never to be the same.

A deeper walk,
less of the talk.

Meekness not weakness,
this is the difference.

Humbly His,
resting in this.

MATTHEW 5:5

⁵ Blessed are the meek,
for they will inherit the earth.

THE LORD'S PEACE

A deeper walk
trusting in Him.
Not to strive
but have peace within.

Overcoming fear
and being in control.
Delivering me
by healing my soul.

PSALMS 42:7

[7] Deep calls to deep in the roar of your waterfalls; all your waves and breakers have swept over me.

EMBRACE ALL OF HIM

Let the love of God,
mark you.

The spirit of God,
change you.

The mind of God,
transform you.

The grace of God,
strengthen you.

2 CORINTHIANS 3:18

[18] And we all, who with unveiled faces contemplate the Lord's glory, are being transformed into his image with ever-increasing glory, which comes from the Lord, who is the Spirit.

A NEW DAY

Loving Jesus
is my goal.
He alone,
heals my soul.

Total surrender
letting Him in.
Onwards and upwards
let the day begin.

2 THESSALONIANS 3:5

⁵ May the Lord direct your hearts into God's love and
Christ's perseverance.

YOUR CALLING

Be who God
has called you to be.
Seek to know Him
and find your destiny.

The safest place
is the centre of His will.
Any other place
is a wilderness still.

2 PETER 1:10

[10] Therefore, my brothers and sisters, make every effort to confirm your calling and election. For if you do these things, you will never stumble.

AT HIS COMMAND

God commands us to love
without the disease to please.
Look to Him
for all your needs.

Friends let you grow
and pray for your best.
Let them go
if your heart's not at rest.

Time is too short
to seek man's opinion.
Follow Christ
and work out your salvation.

GALATIANS 1:10

¹⁰ Am I now trying to win the approval of human beings, or of God? Or am I trying to please people? If I were still trying to please people, I would not be a servant of Christ.

2022 VISION

Your vision,
it's always the best.
Your plan,
then my heart is at rest.

Your guidance,
leading the way.
Your life,
then I won't go astray.

Your heart,
showing compassion.
Your mind,
for Kingdom passion.

Your love,
filling my soul.
Your grace,
making me whole.

EPHESIANS 1:11

[11] In him we were also chosen, having been predestined according to the plan of him who works out everything in conformity with the purpose of his will.

HEAR ME

Are you listening
to My voice,
or trusting the world
to make your choice?

Security is being
surrendered to Me.
I already have
the victory.

No fear in life,
no fear in death.
I've conquered all,
for your eternal rest.

Revelation
through My Word.
Equips the saints
who have endured.

As you see everything
through My eyes.
You surely know that
I *AM* the prize.

PSALMS 141:1-2

¹ I call to you, Lord, come quickly to me;
hear me when I call to you.

² May my prayer be set before you like incense; may the
lifting up of my hands be like the evening sacrifice.

SEEK GOD'S WISDOM

Deception will
lead us astray.
Seek God's wisdom,
trust and pray.

He alone
knows the agenda.
Prepares His people
as their defender.

The battle is His
and it is won.
Look to Jesus
God's precious Son.

PSALMS 119:11-13

¹¹ I have hidden your word in my heart that
I might not sin against you.

¹² Praise be to you, Lord; teach me your decrees.

¹³ With my lips I recount all the laws that
come from your mouth.

JESUS

You led me to the cross
knowing I was lost.

I proclaim you my King
You are my everything.

Nothing can compare
to the love You share.

Bless me to *be* a blessing
to all who are searching.

No human point of view
can steal the truth in You.

PROVERBS 29:18

18 Where there is no revelation, people cast off restraint; but blessed is the one who heeds wisdom's instruction.

LED BY THE SPIRIT

Led by the Spirit
and not the flesh,
is walking like Jesus
in thankfulness.

Nailed to the cross
He speaks to you,
"Forgive them, Father,
they know not what they do."

Faith is birthed
by hearing God's Word.
Spiritual awakening to
know Jesus is Lord.

LUKE 23:34A

34a Jesus said, "Father, forgive them, for they do not know what they are doing."

KEEP FIGHTING

There's a war on truth,
so fight the good fight.
It must be pursued
by shining the light.

Our forefathers fought
for 'freedom of speech'.
Without faith and action,
it's becoming out of reach.

God calls His church
to be awake.
'Woke' is the term
for lives at stake.

That hard-won freedom
paid at a price.
Read the Bible.
Don't fall for the lies.

Obedience to Christ
is our mission.
Surrendered to Him
our only vision.

1 TIMOTHY 6:12

¹² Fight the good fight of the faith. Take hold of the eternal life to which you were called when you made your good confession in the presence of many witnesses.

DON'T JUDGE

Never judge a book by its cover.
God knows our hearts like no other.

In our weakness is His strength.
Our testimony glorifies His defence.

1 SAMUEL 16:7C

7c The Lord does not look at the things people look at.
People look at the outward appearance,
but the Lord looks at the heart."

SET US FREE

When we lead men to the truth
He will set them free.

It is no longer I that lives
but Christ who lives in me.

GALATIANS 2:20

[20] I have been crucified with Christ and I no longer live,
but Christ lives in me. The life I now live in the body,
I live by faith in the Son of God, who loved
me and gave himself for me.

THE CALL

No matter what life throws at me.
I must nail my flesh
to Calvary's tree.

Led by His Spirit every time
is the Christian call
and therefore mine.

ROMANS 8:14

[14] For those who are led by the Spirit of God
are the children of God.

A RACE TO RUN

Asked to run
my own race.
No one else
can take my place.

Yielding to Jesus
all The Way.
To see His face
on that day.

1 CORINTHIANS 9:24

24 Do you not know that in a race all the runners run,
but only one gets the prize?
Run in such a way as to get the prize.

THE JOURNEY

Our journey
is a process.
Seeking truth
in the wilderness.

Only Jesus
can and will,
calm our hearts
to be still.

PSALMS 46:10

¹⁰ He says, "Be still, and know that I am God; I will be exalted among the nations, I will be exalted in the earth."

FAITH IN CHRIST

Faith is not a formula.
It is in Christ alone.
Trust is worship
to Jesus the Son.

God sees our heart
despite all temptation.
If surrendered to Him
we are never forsaken.

He is the King
to whom we must run.
Rest is warfare
the battle is won.

HEBREWS 4:3

[3] Now we who have believed enter that rest,
just as God has said, "So I declared on oath in my anger,
'They shall never enter my rest.'" And yet his works
have been finished since the creation of the world.

WORSHIP

I will worship
in every season.
I will worship for
I have good reason.

I will worship
despite my feelings.
I will worship
to heal my emotions.

I will worship
in thought and prayer.
I will worship
Him everywhere.

I will worship
reading the Word.
I will worship
the living God.

ROMANS 12:1

[1] Therefore, I urge you, brothers and sisters, in view of God's mercy, to offer your bodies as a living sacrifice, holy and pleasing to God—this is your true and proper worship.

HE MAKES ME WHOLE

Life is meaningless
without Jesus.
Only He
can rescue us.

It is the power
of the cross.
Sin will flee
as He delivers us.

He loves us more
than life itself
and gave His *all*
by giving Himself.

GALATIANS 1:3-5

³ Grace and peace to you from God our Father and the Lord Jesus Christ,

⁴ who gave himself for our sins to rescue us from the present evil age, according to the will of our God and Father,

⁵ to whom be glory for ever and ever. Amen.

JESUS IS THE REASON

Jesus is the reason
I've made it this far.
The simple gospel
fighting this war.

No more bondage
and fear in life.
Knowing my Saviour
has paid the price.

He loves me enough
to tell me the truth.
And heals all trauma
from my youth.

Thank you, Jesus
for saving me.
I pray for my friends
and family.

JOHN 18:37

[37] "You are a king, then!" said Pilate. Jesus answered,
"You say that I am a king. In fact, the reason I was born and came
into the world is to testify to the truth. Everyone on the side
of truth listens to me."

LOVE THE LORD

Love the Lord your God with all your heart.
That's the start.

Love the Lord your God with all your soul.
Pursue the goal.

Love the Lord your God with all your mind.
Don't be blind

Love the Lord your God with all your strength.
Pray at length.

MARK 12:30

[30] Love the Lord your God with all your heart and with all your soul and with all your mind and with all your strength.

MOVING ON UP

Onwards and upwards,
this is the call.
Focused on Me
lest you fall.

Singleness
of heart and action.
Fear only Me
for yourself and your children.

Seek Me first
to build the kingdom.
No looking back.
There's work to be done.

JEREMIAH 32:38-41

[38] They will be my people, and I will be their God.

[39] I will give them singleness of heart and action, so that they will always fear me and that all will then go well for them and for their children after them.

[40] I will make an everlasting covenant with them: I will never stop doing good to them, and I will inspire them to fear me, so that they will never turn away from me.

[41] I will rejoice in doing them good and will assuredly plant them in this land with all my heart and soul.

THIS DAY IS YOURS, LORD

We give You this day
in every way.
Teach us to focus
and not go astray.

You rule and reign
over great and small.
Nothing is hidden.
You see it all.

Praise will rise
as You turn the tide.
It shakes the skies,
we will not hide.

You are the King,
heaven and earth are Yours.
Our hearts will sing
as You direct our course.

PSALMS 118:24

²⁴ The Lord has done it this very day;
let us rejoice today and be glad.

WHEN HE RETURNS

Telling the truth
will come at a cost.
This is why I came
and went to the cross.

Remember Me
this Easter time.
Not bunnies that offer
no life like mine.

Deception will lead
your heart astray.
Hell is real
it's not child's play.

My blood cries out
to save all men.
Every eye will see
when I come back again.

REVELATION 1:7

7 "Look, He is coming with the clouds," and "every eye will see him, even those who pierced him"; and all peoples on earth "will mourn because of him."

So shall it be! Amen.

READ HIS WORD

"Do you love Me?"
Jesus asks.
Feed my sheep,
this is your task.

You are not called
to entertain.
But prepare my bride
for My return.

My kingdom
is not of this world.
It's from another place.
Read My Word.

Supernatural strength
is what you need.
No longer yoked
you have been freed.

Do not to the world
remain conformed.
Submit to Me
and be transformed.

JOHN 21:17

¹⁷ The third time He said to him, "Simon son of John, do you love me?" Peter was hurt because Jesus asked him the third time, "Do you love me?" He said, "Lord, you know all things; you know that I love you."

Jesus said, "Feed my sheep.

SEEKING

Heavenly Father
soften my heart.
Walking with You
I am set apart.

Boldly approaching
Your throne of grace.
to release my burdens
and seek Your face.

HEBREWS 4:16

[16] Let us then approach God's throne of grace with confidence, so that we may receive mercy and find grace to help us in our time of need.

GOD'S GLORY

Shame dies on exposure
I don't need to look over my shoulder.

Jesus has the victory
He called me out and walks with me.

Every day, I will confess
No fear in life, no fear in death.

I will share His amazing grace
Calvary's cross dying in our place.

Maranatha, come, Lord Jesus,
Glorify yourself amongst us.

ROMANS 10:11

[11] As Scripture says, "Anyone who believes in him will never be put to shame."

I AM

I Am in control
despite the fight.
I Am never wrong
and always right.

I Am never early
and never late.
I Am calling you
to patiently wait.

I Am turning hearts
back to Me.
I Am opening eyes,
so they can see.

I Am seeking to save
all who are lost.
I Am your God,
now count the cost.

EXODUS 3:14

¹⁴ God said to Moses, "I am who I am. This is what you are to say to the Israelites: 'I am has sent me to you."

SACRIFICED FOR MAN

Jesus gave
His life to redeem us.
And He knows
our every weakness.

He is faithful,
just and true.
Stretched out His arms
to save you.

Will you receive
His gift of grace? Let Him come
and take His place.

HEBREWS 10:14

¹⁴ For by one sacrifice He has made perfect forever those who are being made holy.

JESUS KNOWS

Jesus knows our every weakness.
He gave His life
to redeem us.

He is faithful, just and true.
Stretched out His arms
to save you.

Will you receive His gift of grace?
Let Him come
and take His place.

2 CORINTHIANS 12:9

⁹ But He said to me, "My grace is sufficient for you,
for my power is made perfect in weakness."
Therefore I will boast all the more gladly about my weaknesses,
so that Christ's power may rest on me.

THE KING AND I

The Lord my God,
He beckons me.
Spend time with Him
to set me free.

Out of the world,
delivered from temptation.
I will yield
to His transformation.

Freedom of mind,
body and spirit.
Love abounding
that knows no limit.

No longer a slave
to circumstance.
Dwelling in Christ,
a perfect romance.

[7] So you are no longer a slave, but God's child; and since you are his child, God has made you also an heir.

THE PRICE HE PAID

Seek first the Kingdom
above all else.
Then love your neighbour
as yourself.

It is more blessed
to give than receive.
Extending His grace
to those in need.

We love because
God first loved us.
Giving His Son
to die on the cross.

Ransomed, healed, restored
and forgiven.
Paying the price
to enter Heaven.

MATTHEW 20:26-28

²⁶ Not so with you. Instead, whoever wants to become great among you must be your servant,

²⁷ and whoever wants to be first must be your slave—

²⁸ just as the Son of Man did not come to be served, but to serve, and to give his life as a ransom for many."

HIDDEN

Walking with God,
expect opposition.
The enemy hates
when you transition.

From darkness to light,
fear to freedom.
Living now
in His kingdom.

Hidden in Christ,
faith your shield.
The harvest is ripe.
He owns the field.

MARK 10:29-30

[29] "Truly I tell you," Jesus replied, "no one who has left home or brothers or sisters or mother or father or children or fields for me and the gospel

[30] will fail to receive a hundred times as much in this present age: homes, brothers, sisters, mothers, children and fields— along with persecutions—and in the age to come eternal life.

IN HIS ARMS

I am calm in my Father's arms.
He keeps me safe from all harm.

I will never slip from His grip.
He rescued me from the pit.

Everything hidden He will expose.
No more time to be comatose.

Awakened, strengthened in His grace.
Truly the most exciting place.

He is in control and knows it all.
I trust His plan and hear His call.

MARK 10:16

16 And He took the children in his arms, placed his hands on them and blessed them.

YIELD

Yield to The One
who is in control.
Yield to The One
who guards your soul.

Yield to The One
who calls us by name.
Yield to The One
who heals the lame.

Yield to The One
where faith is found.
Yield to The One
on solid ground.

Yield to The One
the beginning and the end.
Yield to The One
our Saviour and friend.

PSALMS 67:5-7

⁵ May the peoples praise you, God;
may all the peoples praise you.

⁶ The land yields its harvest; God, our God, blesses us.

⁷ May God bless us still,
so that all the ends of the earth will fear him.

LIVE FOR HIM

Stop the cycle
of repetitive sin.
Repent to God,
let Him in.

His power alone
sets us free
Live for Him
in victory.

PHILIPPIANS 1:21

21 For to me, to live is Christ and to die is gain.

TEST OF FAITH

Will you trust Me
in this storm
whilst everything around you
isn't the norm?

It is this testing
that proves of faith.
You are Mine
above all wealth.

Do not let fear
rise in your heart.
But know that I have
set you apart.

It is your choice
to bear My Name
and shine for Me
until I come back again.

HEBREWS 13:5

⁵ Keep your lives free from the love of money and be content with what you have, because God has said, "Never will I leave you; never will I forsake you."

WHAT DO YOU NEED?

Am I all you need
or do you look to man for your seed?

You only see in part.
I know the end from the start.

Let Me show you heaven on earth.
This only comes by receiving new birth.

My Holy Spirit sent from above,
Guiding your path in redeeming love.

I am faithful when you are not.
I cannot deny Myself ... I *am God*.

2 TIMOTHY 2:11-13

[11] Here is a trustworthy saying: If we died with him,
we will also live with him;

[12] if we endure, we will also reign with him.
If we disown him, He will also disown us;

[13] if we are faithless, He remains faithful,
for He cannot disown himself.

HEAR HIS WORD

God's Word
is the seed
If planted in your heart
it's all you need.

Faith comes by hearing
the Word.
Let deaf ears open.
Let them be stirred.

This is a spiritual war,
fought in heaven
before manifesting here.

The victory is only
In Christ.
Let go of your plans
and rest in His.

ROMANS 10:17

¹⁷ Consequently, faith comes from hearing the message, and the message is heard through the word about Christ.

IN GOD I STAND

I am a new creation,
no more in condemnation.
Here in the *Grace* of God, I stand.

I let go of the past
and learn to relax.
Here in the *Peace* of God, I stand.

When God is for me
what can man do to me?
Here in the *Love* of God, I stand.

I pray for strength each day
to trust God and obey.
Here in the *Power* of God, I stand.

2 CORINTHIANS 5:17

17 Therefore, if anyone is in Christ, the new creation has come: The old has gone, the new is here!

MY ALL

I long to be
closer to Thee.
Safe in your arms
away from harm.

You are my refuge
and my strength
You give me
hope and confidence.

The gentle whisper
of your voice.
Holy Spirit,
you are my choice.

To serve you Jesus
the greatest call.
You are my song.
My life ... my *all*.

PSALMS 46:1

¹ God is our refuge and strength,
an ever-present help in trouble.

THE PEACE OF THE LORD

The greatest time to be alive.
To see God move
in our times.

He will reveal who He is.
Amidst the chaos
in which we live.

He reigns over those who are reborn.
And speaks His peace
into our storm.

Trust in His unfailing love.
And seek your help
from above.

COLOSSIANS 3:15

¹⁵ Let the peace of Christ rule in your hearts,
since as members of one body you were called to peace.
And be thankful.

HIS EYES SEE ALL

God's eyes roam
to and fro.
To strengthen those
whose hearts He knows.

Have we turned to Him
for help?
Or do we look to man
or self?

In our weakness is
His strength.
He longs to give
us confidence.

When all else fails
it is a sign.
No one but Jesus
can make us shine.

PSALMS 66:7

⁷ He rules forever by his power, his eyes watch the nations—
let not the rebellious rise up against him.

PRAY

Pray for those who suffer persecution
at the hands of deep corruption.

Pray for justice to prevail
as we intercede and travail.

Pray for joy to be their strength
as the Lord is their defence.

Pray for wisdom in our government
and mercy to triumph over judgement.

HABAKKUK 1:4

⁴ Therefore the law is paralysed, and justice never prevails.
The wicked hem in the righteous, so that justice is perverted.

HAVE NO FEAR

The righteous will
never be shaken. They will be remembered forever
and never forsaken.

They will have no fear of bad news.
Their hearts are steadfast,
trusting in the Good News.

They will have no fear.
Their hearts are secure. They know the Lord
is always near.

No matter
whatever their woes
in the end,
they triumph over their foes.

PSALMS 112:5-8

5 Good will come to those who are generous and lend freely, who conduct their affairs with justice.

6 Surely the righteous will never be shaken; they will be remembered forever.

7 They will have no fear of bad news; their hearts are steadfast, trusting in the Lord.

8 Their hearts are secure, they will have no fear; in the end they will look in triumph on their foes.

VIEW FROM THE TOP

When you seek Him with all your heart
He will set you apart.

Anything that hinders Him
has to go as it is sin.

Onwards and upwards,
one day at a time.

The view from the top
is worth the climb.

PSALMS 24:3-5

³ Who may ascend the mountain of the Lord? Who may stand in his holy place?

⁴ The one who has clean hands and a pure heart, who does not trust in an idol or swear by a false god.

⁵ They will receive blessing from the Lord and vindication from God their Savior.

PREPARATION

God prepares us
for what is ahead.
We are not deceived
if we are Spirit-led.

He leads us through
every wilderness.
Into His promises
and His goodness.

The weapons we fight with
are not carnal.
Pulling down strongholds.
Is where we marvel.

No weapon formed
against us shall prosper.
If we surrender all
at His altar.

AMOS 3:7

[7] Surely the Sovereign Lord does nothing without revealing his plan to his servants the prophets.

KEEP ON

Keep on
keeping on.
One day at a time
fixed on The Son.

Slow down,
be still.
Seek to be in the
centre of His will.

Stand up
share His cup.
The enemies camp
He will blow up.

His strength through
every season of drought.
Rooted in Him
not living in doubt.

2 THESSALONIANS 3:5

⁵ May the Lord direct your hearts into God's love and
Christ's perseverance.

PUSH

We push back darkness
by being In Christ.
There's no such thing as
'just being nice'.

The great deceiver
blinds a mind.
From the glorious Gospel;
it is one of a kind.

It transforms a life
from the inside out.
Giving all immunity
from fear and doubt.

Don't look at the world
and get distressed.
Look to Jesus
and be at rest.

2 THESSALONIANS 3:2-3

[2] And pray that we may be delivered from wicked and evil people, for not everyone has faith.

[3] But the Lord is faithful, and He will strengthen you and protect you from the evil one.

MORE

More of Jesus
less of me.
Only His power
defeats the enemy.

In my weakness
is His strength.
Seeking only
His countenance.

EGO.
Exits God Out.
Victory in Christ
is what life is about.

JOHN 3:29-30

[29] The bride belongs to the bridegroom. The friend who attends the bridegroom waits and listens for him, and is full of joy when He hears the bridegroom's voice. That joy is mine, and it is now complete.

[30] He must become greater; I must become less."

GOD'S PERFECT WAYS

God's ways aren't our ways.
He knows the game Satan plays.
Suddenly He can answer your prayer,
anytime and anywhere.

The prayers of a righteous man
avail much.
Guard your heart
from temptation's clutch.

Just one touch
from The King.
Always changes
everything.

JAMES 4:6

⁶ But He gives us more grace.
That is why Scripture says:
"God opposes the proud but shows favour to the humble."

PERFECT

NO FEAR

Never fear
Jesus is near.
If we look to Him
for freedom
from sin.

No one loves us
like He does.
He showed us all
by Calvary's call.

God calls us home
when this life is done.
If we receive
His only Son.

JOHN 14:23

[23] Jesus replied, "Anyone who loves me will obey my teaching. My Father will love them, and we will come to them and make our home with them.

CALLED HOME

I know that Jesus
You hold my hand.
All other ground is sinking sand.

My life is hidden
now in Christ.
Paid for by Your sacrifice.

Calvary the victory.
The greatest day
In history.

Not my will
but Yours be done.
Until You call me home to Heaven.

MATTHEW 7:26-27

26 But everyone who hears these words of mine and does not put them into practice is like a foolish man who built his house on sand.

27 The rain came down, the streams rose, and the winds blew and beat against that house, and it fell with a great crash."

WALK WITH GOD

If we walk
with the Lord, we cannot
conform
to this world.

There is a cost
to follow Christ.
It means we stand
against the lies.

Wait on Me
for My perfect time.
I always deliver
each child of mine.

Fix your eyes
on Me alone.
I never let go
of those I own.

Release your fears
and faith will rise.
The battle is Mine
bringing Satan's demise

PROVERBS 8:34-35

[34] Blessed are those who listen to me, watching daily at my doors, waiting at my doorway.

[35] For those who find me find life and receive favor from the Lord.

WILDERNESS

Are you in
the wilderness?
Look to Me,
don't be distressed.

Read the Word.
Feed your soul.
Knowing Jesus
is your goal.

Count your blessings
every day.
Holy Spirit will
lead the way.

HEBREWS 3:7-8

⁷ So, as the Holy Spirit says: "Today, if you hear his voice,

⁸ do not harden your hearts as you did in the rebellion, during the time of testing in the wilderness.

WISDOM

God grant us wisdom
in these days.
Cause us to rise
above the waves.

Teach us sound doctrine
found in Your Word.
Renew our minds
from all that's absurd.

Help us protect children
from indoctrination.
Stand against the agenda,
our moral obligation.

1 TIMOTHY 4:1

[1] The Spirit clearly says that in later times some will abandon the faith and follow deceiving spirits and things taught by demons.

SELFLESS

Love thy neighbour
as thyself.
Blessing others
before yourself.

1 PETER 3:9

⁹ Do not repay evil with evil or insult with insult. On the contrary, repay evil with blessing, because to this you were called so that you may inherit a blessing.

WAKE UP

First things first,
His Kingdom come.
In our lives
Thy will be done.

Wake up, wake up!
Life awaits.
Don't waste time
at the enemy's gates.

Taste and see
that the Lord is good.
Give us today
our daily food.

Don't blame Him
for sin and its curse.
He died in your place
to maintain the reverse.

Blessings and honour,
glory and power.
Offered today
in this hour.

REVELATION 16:15

15 "Look, I come like a thief? Blessed is the one who stays awake and remains clothed, so as not to go naked and be shamefully exposed."

INNOCENCE

Will you choose to make a difference?
Protect our children and their innocence?

Is your trust in mainstream media?
Are you awake to the world's agenda?

It is in Christ we are set free
not yoked again to slavery.

Our sword is truth of God's Word
not returning void as Jesus is Lord.

ROMANS 16:17-19

[17] I urge you, brothers and sisters, to watch out for those who cause divisions and put obstacles in your way that are contrary to the teaching you have learned. Keep away from them.

[18] For such people are not serving our Lord Christ, but their own appetites. By smooth talk and flattery they deceive the minds of naive people.

[19] Everyone has heard about your obedience, so I rejoice because of you; but I want you to be wise about what is good, and innocent about what is evil.

AUTHORITY

Those in authority
in the spotlight,
failing children
out of sight.

It's time corruption
is exposed;
to rescue
every one of those.

Love compels
me every day
to step out in faith
and make a way.

ROMANS 1:18

[18] The wrath of God is being revealed from heaven against all the godlessness and wickedness of people, who suppress the truth by their wickedness.

SPEAK UP

Speak up for nature with climate change.
Yet silence for the abused "in Satan's name?"

"Be quiet!" you say
"It's hard to hear."
Rescue the children who live in fear.

Halloween approaching.
Children having fun?
Choose this day.
Whose side you're on?

JOSHUA 24:15

[15] But if serving the Lord seems undesirable to you, then choose for yourselves this day whom you will serve, whether the gods your ancestors served beyond the Euphrates or the gods of the Amorites, in whose land you are living. But as for me and my household, we will serve the Lord."

OLDER

As I get older
and hopefully wiser,
all of life's struggles
push me further.

To find my Identity
in Christ alone.
He has become
the Cornerstone.

Faith over fear
at every hurdle.
Not cowering under
the weight of turmoil.

MATTHEW 21:42

⁴² Jesus said to them, "Have you never read in the Scriptures:
"The stone the builders rejected has become the cornerstone;
the Lord has done this,
and it is marvellous in our eyes?"

TRUTH

In all the chaos and confusion,
where is Truth
and the solution?

Be sensitive to those in pain.
God sees their hearts and knows their name.

Religion binds but Jesus sets free.
That's why He says, "All come to Me."

His yoke is easy, His burden is light.
Let Him help us to fight the good fight.

GALATIANS 1:6-7

⁶ I am astonished that you are so quickly deserting the one who called you to live in the grace of Christ and are turning to a different gospel—

⁷ which is really no gospel at all. Evidently, some people are throwing you into confusion and are trying to pervert the gospel of Christ.

HERE I COME

Get ready because
here I come.
Wash your robes
to enter The Kingdom.

I AM holy.
Awake and see
Repent from sin
to abide in Me.

It is my free gift
the water of life.
Washing away
all pain and strife.

Humble yourselves under
my mighty hand.
My Spirit will fill you with
grace to stand.

REVELATION 7:13-17

[13] Then one of the elders asked me, "These in white robes—
who are they, and where did they come from?"

[14] I answered, "Sir, you know. "And he said, "These are they
who have come out of the great tribulation; they have washed
their robes and made them white in the blood of the Lamb.

[15] Therefore, "they are before the throne of God and serve
him day and night in his temple; and he who sits on the
throne will shelter them with his presence.

[16] 'Never again will they hunger; never again will they thirst.
The sun will not beat down on them, 'nor any scorching heat.

[17] For the Lamb at the center of the throne will be their
shepherd; "He will lead them to springs of living water.
And God will wipe away every tear from their eyes."

PROTECTION

Protect the Children.
I've shared my story for many years.
To protect the children
and wipe away their tears.

The truth is now
being exposed.
I know the pain
I was one of those.

My cry was desperate
to be saved.
Jesus rescued me
from the grave.

He put a new song
in my mouth,
a hymn of praise,
no longer in doubt

Unconditionally loved,
no longer a slave.
My destiny planned,
forever saved.

PSALMS 40:1-3

¹ I waited patiently for the Lord;
he turned to me and heard my cry.

² He lifted me out of the slimy pit, out of the mud and mire;
he set my feet on a rock and gave me a firm place to stand.

³ He put a new song in my mouth,
a hymn of praise to our God.
Many will see and fear the Lord and put their trust in him.

MESSAGE TO THE READER

Never doubt yourself on
how far you have come.
Despite the fight,
faith has won.
Amen.

Many SRA Survivors are now speaking out all over the world, corroborating all that I have endeavoured to disclose all these years. Many have been and are being silenced by fear and imprisonment due to the corruption in high places run by elite satanic paedophiles.

Evil only prospers when good men do nothing. The devil only prospers when God's men do nothing therefore, fight the good fight of faith to the very end.

ABOUT THE AUTHOR

Author Vicky Ash is a Satanic Ritual Abuse (SRA) survivor and campaigns tirelessly for exposure to protect innocent children.

She has spoken out extensively since the 1990s and given many interviews on television, radio and social media platforms.

Satanism is endemic in our society and 'evil only prospers when good men do nothing.'

She is married to Chris who she met in her teenage years and has three grown-up children; two sons, one daughter with an Autistic Spectrum Disorder and three grandchildren.

She is the proprietor of Christoria Christian Outreach and Community Hub.

Her passion is to help people to find their Freedom In Christ, not letting past abuse and its symptoms keep one in bondage.

She is a qualified Beauty Therapist and keep-fit instructor using these skills at Christoria. She was diagnosed with Systemic Lupus Erythematosus (SLE) in her early thirties. Despite much adversity, she experiences daily that in her weakness is His strength.

2 CORINTHIANS 12:9 -10

⁹ But he said to me, "My grace is sufficient for you,
for my power is made perfect in weakness." Therefore
I will boast all the more gladly about my weaknesses,
so that Christ's power may rest on me.

¹⁰ That is why, for Christ's sake, I delight in weaknesses,
in insults, in hardships, in persecutions, in difficulties.
For when I am weak, then I am strong.

REVIEW ASK

Thank you for reading this book and I hope that you enjoyed it.
Don't forget to head over to Amazon and a leave a review!
Thank you so much.

Get in touch with Vicky Ash

Email: christoriaffl@hotmail.com

Printed in Great Britain
by Amazon

16978551R00132